Copyright 2020 by Mark Briggs -All rights reserved.

No part of this publication may be reproduced, distributed, or transmitted in any form or by any means, including photocopying, recording, or other electronic or mechanical methods, without the prior written permission of the publisher, except in the case of brief quotations embodied in reviews and certain other non-commercial uses permitted by copyright law.

This Book is provided with the sole purpose of providing relevant information on a specific topic for which every reasonable effort has been made to ensure that it is both accurate and reasonable. Nevertheless, by purchasing this Book you consent to the fact that the author, as well as the publisher, are in no way experts on the topics contained herein, regardless of any claims as such that may be made within. It is recommended that you always consult a professional prior to undertaking any of the advice or techniques discussed within. This is a legally binding declaration that is considered both valid and fair by both the Committee of Publishers Association and the American Bar Association and should be considered as legally binding within the United States.

CONTENTS

Introduction 7
    What Is The Optavia Diet? 7
    The Benefits Of The Optavia Diet 7
    What To Eat? 8
    What Not To Eat 9
    Why The Air Fryer Is Great For The Optavia Diet 10
    Tips And Tricks To Using Air Fryer With Optavia Diet 12

Optavia Diet Lean and Green Air Fryed Chicken Recipes 14
    Simple Air Fried Chicken Strips 14
    Mediterranean Chicken Salad 15
    Baked Chipotle Chicken 16
    Chicken Lettuce Wraps 17
    Chicken and Cauliflower Mini Casserole 18
    Pesto Air Fried Chicken 19
    Baked Chicken and Zucchini Casserole 20
    Arroz Con Pollo 21
    Chicken Tzatziki 22
    Chicken Cobb Salad 23
    Chicken Loaf with Fennel 24
    Spicy Air Fried Chicken 25
    Air Fried Chicken Tenders 26
    Air Fried Whole Chicken Rotisserie Style 27
    Lean and Green Garlic Chicken 28
    Air Fryer Mustard Chicken 29
    Air Fried Korean Chicken 30
    Air Fried Chicken and Broccoli 31

Air Fried Ginger and Lemon Grass Chicken 32

Air Fryer Rosemary Chicken Breast 33

Optavia Diet Lean and Green Air Fryed Vegetarian Recipes 34

Air Fried Crispy Vegetables 34

Air Fried Broccoli 35

Air Fried Roasted Asparagus 36

Air Fried Collard Greens 37

Air Fried Mushrooms 38

Thai Asparagus, Kale, And Garlic Mushrooms 39

Air Fried Asparagus Fries 40

Collard Chips 41

Air Fryer Artichoke 42

Air Fried Eggplants 43

Spicy Air Fried Eggplant 44

Air Fryer Butternut Squash Fries 45

Air Fried Cinnamon Butternut Squash 46

Air Fried Swiss Chard Chips 47

Air Fried Roasted Cauliflower 48

Air Fried Roasted Broccoli and Cauliflower 49

Roasted Purple Cauliflower 50

Air Fryer Kale Chips 51

Air Fried Roasted Tomatoes 52

Air Fryer Stuffed Tomatoes 53

Salt and Vinegar Spinach Chips 54

Kohlrabi Chips 55

Spicy Kohlrabi Fries 56

Daikon Chips 57

Air Fried Roasted Peppers 58

Optavia Diet Lean and Green Air Fryed Beef, Pork and Meat Recipes 59

Air Fryer Meat Loaf 59

Air Fryer Roasted Beef 60

Air Fried Burger Patties 61

Air Fried Rib Eye Steak 62

Air Fryer Steak Bites and Mushrooms 63

Air Fried Lamb Chops 64

Air Fried Roasted Lamb 65

Roast Lamb Rack 66

Air Fried Masala Chops 67

Mutton Chops 68

Rosemary Crusted Lamb Chops 69

Air Fryer Pork Chops 70

Air Fryer Pork Tenderloin 71

Mustard Pork Chops 72

Air Fryer Italian Pork Chops 73

Air Fried Riblets 74

Pork Tenderloin with Fried Bell Peppers 75

Air Fried Beef Jerky 76

Air Fried Pot Roast 77

Air Fried Mongolian Beef 78

Optavia Diet Lean and Green Air Fryed Seafood Recipes 79

Air Fried Scallops 79

Air Fried Salmon 80

Air Fryer Cajun Crab Legs 81

Air Fried Crab Cakes 82

Air Fried Blackened Flounder 83

Air Fried Tuna Steaks 84

Simple Air Fried Tuna Steak 85

Almond Crusted Fried Masala Fish 86

Thai-Style Fish Fillet 87

Ginger Tuna Steak with Charred Green Scallions 88

Air Fried Roasted Tuna with Dill 89

Air Fried Lemon Pepper Shrimps 90

Air Fryer Spicy Garlic Shrimps with Lemon and Dill 91

Air Fried Blackened Tilapia 92

Air Fryer Cod 93

Air Fried Halibut 94

Air Fried White Fish with Garlic and Lemon En Papillote 95

Air Fried Crispy Fish Skins 96

Thai Grilled Fish 97

Air Fried Fish Fillets with Basil and Garlic Puree 98

Optavia Diet Air Fryer Fueling Recipes 99

Mustard Chicken Nuggets 99

Smashed Potato Grilled Cheese 100

Silky Peanut Butter Cookies 101

Buffalo Cauliflower Wings 102

Sweet Potato Goat Cheese and Rosemary Quiche Cups 103

Peanut Butter Brownie Whoopie Pies 104

Cheesy Spinach Smashed Potatoes 105

Chocolate Chip Cake 106

Mini Cranberry Orange Spiced Cheesecake 107

French Toast Sticks 108

Blueberry Almond Scones 109

Sweet Potato Pecan Muffins 110

Air Fried Shake Cake 111

Pumpkin Chocolate Cheesecake.. 112

Cinnamon Bun Blondies... 113

Introduction

What Is The Optavia Diet?

The Optavia Diet, also known as the Medifast Diet, this particular diet regimen was developed by Dr. William Vitale in the 1980s. His products were first sold directly to his fellow doctors who, in turn, prescribe them to their patients. Eventually, he made his products and developed what is Optavia Diet now in order for a wider audience to access his products.The Optavia Diet is a meal replacement diet that basically removes all the guesswork involved in successful dieting. As a meal replacement diet, it encourages dieters to consume proprietary products that can aid people in weight loss and, at the same time, never lose energy to sustain their daily activities.Under this particular diet regimen, dieters are strictly encouraged to follow a weight plan that usually includes five fuelings a day and one lean green meal. This is their 5&1 diet plan. But depending on your needs, the Optavia Diet comes with other diet plans that you can adapt. The diet plan is designed to keep you healthy thus making it a perfect diet regimen for everyone considering that everyone has specific diet and energy needs.But because the Optavia Diet is a commercial diet, dieters need to buy the Optavia fuelings in order to follow their weight plan. Nevertheless, this is one of the most successful diet regimens to date as it is backed by decades of scientific studies.

The Benefits Of The Optavia Diet

The Optavia Diet has a high success rate in terms of weight loss and management. But aside from helping everyone achieve their ideal weight, there is more to Optavia Diet in terms of the benefits that it can give to people. Below are the benefits of the Optavia Diet. And if you are still not following the diet regimen, then this list will definitely attract you to follow this diet.

- **Structured eating plan:** One of the biggest reasons why people fail to succeed with any diet plans is that they do not have discipline. The Optavia Diet enforces good eating habits as it features a structured eating plan. This means that you have to strictly follow what is indicated on their website and lapses are frowned upon by the Optavia Diet community.
- **Better portion control:** Portion control is what drives the Optavia Diet plans. The many Optavia Diet plans is strict with its fueling phase. You need to eat what is specified in your fuelings pack.
- **Supportive community:** Many people do not have a good relationship with food. This is the reason why so many people revert to their old eating habits. With the Optavia Diet, not only are you backed with a helping and supporting community that will always encourage you to eat healthily. Given the support that you will get from the community, it is easier for you to follow the diet plans as you gain an appreciation not only for food but also for the camaraderie of your fellow dieters.
- **Better overall wellness:** This diet regimen encourages you to eat healthily. Since the Optavia Diet frowns upon the intake of too much sodium, it promotes better cardiovascular health.

What To Eat?

While there are many Optavia Diet plans that dieters can choose from, one thing is for certain and that is dieters are encouraged to consume lean proteins and non-starchy vegetables. In some ways, the Optavia Diet requires you to restrict eating certain food groups but only because these food groups will not help you achieve your health goals. And while it is somehow restrictive, there are still so many types of foods that you can enjoy while following this diet regimen. Below is a list of foods that you are allowed to eat while following this diet regimen.

- **Optavia fuelings:** The Optavia Diet encourages dieters to consume prepackaged Optavia fueling foods. The company has more than 60 shakes, bars, soups, and fueling products that you can use as meal replacements. Eat them during your fueling phase.
- **Green and non-starchy foods:** These foods do not contain high amounts of carbohydrates so they do not interfere with your weight loss. However, they are still categorized into the following:
- **Low carb:** All types of salad greens as well as leafy green vegetables.
- **Moderate carb:** Summer squash and cauliflower.
- **Higher carb:** Peppers and broccoli.
- **Lean meats:** Lean meats are necessary for your lean and green phase. But similar to the vegetables, they are also classified according to their fat content as follows:
- **Lean:** Lean meats include salmon, lamb, and pork chops.
- **Leaner:** These include swordfish and chicken breasts.
- **Leanest:** These include egg whites, cod, and shrimps
- **Healthy fats:** Healthy fats include walnut oil, olive oil, flaxseed, and avocado. Make sure to consume at least two servings of healthy fats to meet your daily requirements.
- **Others:** As soon as you have already achieved your ideal weight loss goals, you can start consuming other heavy foods to maintain your weight. These include low-fat dairy, whole grains, and fresh fruits.

What Not To Eat

The Optavia Diet is similar to other diet regimens such that it discourages the consumption of certain types of foods that will keep you off the track towards healthy eating and achieving your weight loss goals. Below are the foods that you should avoid while following the Optavia Diet:

- **Sugary drinks:** Sugary drinks such as soda (diet and normal) are high in sugar. Make sure that you stay away from them. Other sugary drinks that you need to avoid are fruit juices and energy drinks. If you can help it, drink water instead.
- **Indulgent desserts:** Indulgent desserts such as ice cream, cakes, and other sweet pastries are loaded with sugar. If you want to indulge your sweet teeth, you can always go for fresh fruits and yogurt. However, make sure that you restrict the consumption of fruits and vegetables a few weeks after you have achieved your ideal weight.
- **Alcohol:** Limit your alcohol intake to 5 ounces of alcohol daily. The reason why you need to limit your alcohol intake is that alcohol, even in small amounts, are high in calories.
- **Unhealthy fats:** Unhealthy fats like shortening, butter, and commercial salad dressing contains high amounts of calories. This is not good especially if you are trying to lose weight. Moreover, these commercial fats also come with a lot of preservatives particularly salt that is not good for the health.

Why The Air Fryer Is Great For The Optavia Diet

The air fryer is one of the most intuitive kitchen appliances that you can own. In fact, this is the trendiest kitchen appliance that anyone can own. It comes with preset cooking functions that allow you to cook different kinds of foods from whole fried chicken to cakes in just a touch of a finger. With this digital fryer, you remove all the guesswork when cooking food thus you can cook complicated food even if you are a kitchen neophyte.

But aside from kitchen neophytes, the air fryer is perfect among people who are following a particular diet regimen. People who follow the Optavia Diet are more likely to benefit from investing in an air fryer. So how can followers of the Optavia Diet benefit from air fryers? Read on to understand why the air fryer is great for Optavia Diet.

- **May help in weight loss:** The reason why the air fryer is designed is to allow people to eat their favorite comfort foods minus the grease and fat. The Optavia Diet requires dieters to consume only 5 ounces of healthy fats daily. By owning an air fryer, you will still be able to eat your favorite comfort foods because you now have a way to cook them minus the oil.
- **Faster cooking time:** Many people cannot keep up with their diet regimen because they do not have the luxury of time to slave in the kitchen cooking healthy foods. Air fryers are designed to have a convection cooking mechanism. The hot air that gets circulated all over the cooking chamber or fryer basket thus resulting in faster cooking time. Convenience and ease are the two selling points of the air fryers. Dieters will naturally patronize air fryers because they can cook food faster so they can spend more of their time doing other equally more important things.
- **Practical kitchen device:** Another reason why the Air Fryer is perfect for those who follow the Optavia Diet is that it is a practical kitchen device. Because the air fryer allows you to cook not only fried foods but even bake in them, you will be able to make a wide variety of foods. Most people find it off-putting to follow a certain diet regimen because they think that they have limited preparations for their meals. With the air fryer, your Optavia-approved meals will never be boring.
- **Less messy:** There is little mess involved when cooking with an air fryer. Since food is cooked inside a chamber, gone are the days when you have to clean the kitchen counter from oil splatter. On the other hand, even if you do not use

oil in cooking your food, your food comes out more flavorful because the circulating air allows the flavor to circulate all over your food. For people who follow the Optavia Diet, being able to cook very flavorful food is a good advantage. You simply eat good food with an air fryer minus the guilt.

Tips And Tricks To Using Air Fryer With Optavia Diet

Being able to successfully make Optavia-approved meals with an air fryer is very much possible. While air fryers are very easy to operate, some people might find it challenging. This is especially true among kitchen neophytes. Thus, below are tips on how to use the air fryer and maximize its use.

- **Get to know your air fryer:** Before you start using your air fryer, it is important to read the user manual particularly on the safety and cooking instructions. Do not use the machine inappropriately to avoid damaging your kitchen device. This will also allow you to know the perfect settings that you can use to cook different types of foods.
- **Always cook in batches:** If you are going to cook large amounts of foods, make sure that you cook in batches. The problem with putting everything in the fryer basket is that the hot air will not be able to circulate all your food. This will lead to your food not cooking evenly.
- **Use the right accessories:** If you want to extend the functionality of your air fryer, make sure that you invest in the right accessories. Air fryers come with a wide array of accessories. These include baking pans, grill pans, and cooking rack with skewers. Use the baking pans to cook different types of pastries and desserts using your air fryer. However, make sure that the baking pan will fit inside the air fryer properly. On the other hand, you can use the grill pans to create perfect grilled marks on your food. Lastly, use skewers to make different types of skewered foods.

- **Clean up after using:** Cleaning your air fryer daily is very important. As the grease present inside the air fryer chamber can be exposed to higher heat during future cooking. This will eventually lead to burning and smoking that may affect the overall flavor profile of your foods.

Optavia Diet Lean and Green Air Fryed Chicken Recipes

Simple Air Fried Chicken Strips

Servings: 4

Cooking Time: 20 minutes

Ingredients:

2 pounds chicken breasts, skin removed and sliced into thick strips

A dash of salt and pepper

Cooking spray

Directions:

1) Preheat the air fryer to 350^0F for five minutes.
2) Place the chicken in a bowl and season with salt and pepper to taste.
3) Toss to season all chicken strips.
4) Spray with cooking oil.
5) Place inside the air fryer basket and cook for 20 minutes.
6) Make sure to give the basket a shake halfway through the cooking time for even cooking.
7) Cook in batches if necessary.

Nutrition Information: Calories per serving: 210; Protein: 50g; Carbs:3 g; Fat:2 g Sugar: 0g

Mediterranean Chicken Salad

Servings: 2

Cooking Time: 25minutes

Ingredients:

1 ¾ pounds boneless chicken breasts, cut into strips

¼ teaspoon salt

1/8 teaspoon pepper

6 cups romaine lettuce

1 cup sliced cucumber

1-pint cherry tomatoes, halved

1 small lemon, juice

Directions:

1) Preheat the air fryer to 350^0F for five minutes.
2) Place the chicken in a bowl and season with salt and pepper to taste.
3) Toss to season all chicken strips.
4) Spray with cooking oil.
5) Place inside the air fryer basket and cook for 20 minutes.
6) Make sure to give the basket a shake halfway through the cooking time for even cooking.
7) Set aside to cool.
8) Place the lettuce, cucumber, and tomatoes in a bowl.
9) Season with lemon juice and salt. Toss to coat the vegetables with the seasoning.
10) Add in chicken strips last.
11) Cook in batches if necessary.

Nutrition Information: Calories per serving: 272; Protein: 53g; Carbs: 3g; Fat: 2g Sugar: 1g

Baked Chipotle Chicken

Servings: 4

Cooking Time: 30 minutes

Ingredients:

1 cup tomatoes, sliced

¼ cup dried chipotle peppers, chopped

1 teaspoon cumin

½ teaspoon dried oregano

¼ teaspoon salt

1 ½ pounds boneless chicken breasts, skin removed

Directions:

1) Preheat the air fryer to 350^0F for five minutes.

2) Place in a food processor the tomatoes, chipotle peppers, cumin, oregano, and salt. Pulse until smooth.

3) Place the chicken in a heat-proof dish that will fit inside the air fryer basket.

4) Pour over the chipotle sauce.

5) Place the dish inside the baking tray.

6) Cook for 30 minutes.

7) Cook in batches if necessary.

Nutrition Information: Calories per serving: 256; Protein: 35g; Carbs: 3g; Fat: 2g Sugar: 1g

Chicken Lettuce Wraps

Servings: 4

Cooking Time: 20 minutes

Ingredients:

1-pound chicken breasts, sliced into strips

A dash and pepper to taste

2 teaspoons fajita seasoning

Cooking spray

6 leaves of romaine lettuce

2 bell peppers, seeded and julienned

Juice from ½ lime

Directions:

1) Preheat the air fryer to 350^0F for five minutes.
2) Place the chicken in a bowl and season with salt and pepper to taste. Add in the fajita seasoning.
3) Toss to season all chicken strips.
4) Spray with cooking oil.
5) Place inside the air fryer basket and cook for 20 minutes.
6) Give the air fryer basket a little shake for even cooking.
7) Cook in batches if necessary.
8) Once cooked, allow the chicken to cool.
9) Assemble the fajita.
10) Place chicken pieces in romaine lettuce and top with bell pepper.
11) Season with salt and lime juice.

Nutrition Information: Calories per serving: 237; Protein: 25g; Carbs: 5g; Fat: 2g Sugar: 1g

Chicken and Cauliflower Mini Casserole

Servings: 4

Cooking Time: 25 minutes

Ingredients:

2 cloves of garlic, minced

2 pounds chicken breasts, minced

1 cup cauliflower florets, chopped

½ teaspoons dried oregano

2 scallions, chopped

Salt and pepper to taste

Directions:

1) Preheat the air fryer to 350°F for five minutes.

2) Place in a heat-proof dish all ingredients. Stir to combine. Make sure that the casserole dish will fit inside the air fryer basket.

3) Put the casserole dish in the air fryer.

4) Air fry for 25 minutes.

5) Cook in batches if necessary.

Nutrition Information: Calories per serving: 245; Protein: 35g; Carbs: 10g; Fat: 2g Sugar: 3g

Pesto Air Fried Chicken

Servings: 4

Cooking Time: 30 minutes

Ingredients:

1/3 cup fresh basil

½ ounce almond nuts

Salt to taste

Juice from ½ lemon

1 ½ pounds boneless chicken breasts, cubed

½ cup cherry tomatoes, halved

½ teaspoon crushed red pepper flakes

Directions:

1) Preheat the air fryer to $350°F$ for five minutes.
2) Place the basil, almond, salt, and lemon juice in a food processor. Pulse until smooth. Set aside.
3) Place the chicken breasts in a heat-proof dish. Make sure that it will fit inside the air fryer basket.
4) Pour over the pesto sauce.
5) Place the tomatoes in the casserole and garnish with red pepper flakes.
6) Place the casserole dish in the air fryer basket.
7) Cook for 30 minutes.
8) Cook in batches if necessary.

Nutrition Information: Calories per serving: 235; Protein: 33.2g; Carbs: 10g; Fat: 2g Sugar: 2g

Baked Chicken and Zucchini Casserole

Servings: 4

Cooking Time: 30 minutes

Ingredients:

1 ¾ pounds boneless chicken breasts, cubed

¼ teaspoon garlic powder

¼ teaspoon salt

¼ teaspoon pepper

½ cup diced zucchini

½ cup cashew or almond milk

1 teaspoon basil leaves, chopped

1 teaspoon oregano, chopped

Directions:

1)   Preheat the air fryer to 350°F for five minutes.

2)   Place all ingredients in a heat-proof dish. Make sure that the heat-proof dish will fit inside the air fryer basket.

3)   Cook in batches if necessary.

4)   Place the casserole dish inside the air fryer basket.

5)   Cook for 30 minutes.

Nutrition Information: Calories per serving: 273; Protein: 35g; Carbs: 5g; Fat: 7g Sugar: 1g

Arroz Con Pollo

Servings: 4

Cooking Time: 20 minutes

Ingredients:

1 ¾ boneless chicken breasts, cubed

Salt and pepper to taste

1 scallion, minced

2 cups grated cauliflower, blanched

1 ½ cups cherry tomatoes, halved

½ cup green beans, cut into ¼ inch pieces and blanched

Directions:

1) Preheat the air fryer to 350°F for five minutes.

2) Season the chicken with salt and pepper to taste and place inside the air fryer basket.

3) Cook for 20 minutes. Make sure that you give the air fryer basket a shake for even cooking.

4) Serve the chicken with blanched cauliflower, tomatoes, and beans.

5) Season with salt and pepper if necessary.

Nutrition Information: Calories per serving: 214; Protein: 37g; Carbs:8 g; Fat: 2g Sugar: 3g

Chicken Tzatziki

Servings: 4

Cooking Time: 25 minutes

Ingredients:

1-pound boneless chicken breasts, cut into strips

Salt and pepper to taste

½ cup grated cucumber

½ cup low-fat Greek yogurt, plain

½ cup crushed garlic

Directions:

1) Preheat the air fryer to 350^0F for five minutes.

2) Season with salt and pepper to taste. Spray with cooking oil.

3) Place inside the air fryer basket. Cook for 25 minutes. Make sure to give the air fryer basket a good shake for even cooking.

4) Meanwhile, mix the cucumber, yogurt, and garlic in a bowl.

5) Serve the chicken with the sauce.

Nutrition Information: Calories per serving: 283; Protein: 30g; Carbs: 15g; Fat: 4g Sugar: 5g

Chicken Cobb Salad

Servings: 2

Cooking Time: 20 minutes

Ingredients:

1-pound chicken breasts, cut into strips

Salt and pepper to taste

Cooking spray

4 cups romaine lettuce, torn

2 hard-boiled egg, white part only

1 cup cherry tomatoes, halved

2 tablespoons avocado, mashed

3 tablespoons reduce Sodium ranch dressing

Directions:

1) Preheat the air fryer to 350^0F for five minutes.

2) Season with salt and pepper to taste. Spray with cooking oil.

3) Place inside the air fryer basket. Cook for 20 minutes. Make sure to give the air fryer basket a good shake for even cooking. Set aside the cooked chicken.

4) Assemble the cobb salad by placing the lettuce in a salad bowl. Add the egg, tomatoes, and avocado. Add the chicken strips.

5) Season with salt and pepper as well as the ranch dressing.

Nutrition Information: Calories per serving: 325; Protein: 43g; Carbs: 18g; Fat: 9g Sugar: 2g

Chicken Loaf with Fennel

Servings: 6

Cooking Time: 30 minutes

Ingredients:

2 pounds chicken breasts, ground

2 cups chopped cabbage

2 green onions, chopped

¼ cup pine nuts, toasted then crushed

1 teaspoon paprika

1 teaspoon salt, divided

1 teaspoon black pepper

1 tablespoon olive oil

2 small fennel bulbs, finely chopped

Directions:

1) Preheat the air fryer to 350°F for five minutes.
2) Combine all ingredients in a bowl. Mix until well-combined.
3) Place in a small loaf pan that will fit inside the air fryer basket.
4) Place the pan inside the air fryer and cook for 30 minutes.
5) Cook in batches if necessary.

Nutrition Information: Calories per serving: 300; Protein 41 g; Carbs: 14g; Fat: 4g Sugar: 6g

Spicy Air Fried Chicken

Servings: 5

Cooking Time: 20 minutes

Ingredients:

5 large chicken thighs, skin removed

1 tablespoon soy sauce

1 tablespoon sesame oil

1 clove of garlic, minced

¾ teaspoon crushed red pepper flakes

Directions:

1) Place all ingredients in a bowl and allow the chicken to marinate for 2 hours inside the fridge.

2) Preheat the air fryer to 350^0F for five minutes.

3) Place the chicken pieces inside the air fryer basket.

4) Cook for 20 minutes.

5) Make sure that you give the air fryer basket a shake halfway through the cooking time for even cooking.

Nutrition Information: Calories per serving: 288; Protein: 25g; Carbs: 1g; Fat: 4g Sugar:0.1 g

Air Fried Chicken Tenders

Servings: 4

Cooking Time: 20 minutes

Ingredients:

¼ cup unsweetened coconut, shredded

¼ cup coconut flour

½ cup almond meal

1 teaspoon pepper

1 egg white, beaten

1 tablespoon almond milk

1-pound chicken breasts, cut into strips

Salt and pepper to taste

Directions:

1) Preheat the air fryer to 450^0F for five minutes.

2) In a bowl, mix the shredded coconut, coconut flour, almond meal, and pepper.

3) In another bowl, mix the egg and milk.

4) Season the chicken with salt and pepper to taste

5) Dip the chicken strips in the egg mixture and dredge in the coconut mixture.

6) Place the chicken in the air fryer basket. Leave enough room for the air to circulate. If cramped, cook in batches.

7) Cook for 20 minutes. Give the air fryer basket a shake for even cooking.

Nutrition Information: Calories per serving: 300; Protein: 30g; Carbs:9 g; Fat: 10g Sugar: 2g

Air Fried Whole Chicken Rotisserie Style

Servings: 6

Cooking Time: 1 hour

Ingredients:

2 tablespoons avocado oil

1 tablespoon salt

1 teaspoon ground pepper to taste

1 teaspoon garlic powder

½ teaspoon dried basil

½ teaspoon dried oregano

1 5 pounds whole chicken, giblets removed

Directions:

1) Preheat the air fryer to 340°F for five minutes.

2) Combine all seasonings to create a paste.

3) Rub the paste all over the chicken and allow to rest for 10 minutes.

4) Place chicken in the air fryer basket. Cover top of chicken with foil and set in place by inserting a toothpick. Remove the foil 50 minutes into the cooking time.

5) Cook for 60 minutes and let chicken rest for at least 5 minutes before carving.

Nutrition Information: Calories per serving: 294; Protein: 50.6g; Carbs: 4g; Fat: 3g Sugar: 0.4g

Lean and Green Garlic Chicken

Servings: 3

Cooking Time: 30 minutes

Ingredients:

1 ½ tablespoons boneless skinless chicken breasts

1 cup low fat plain Greek yogurt

½ teaspoon garlic powder

½ teaspoon Italian seasoning

3 cloves of garlic, minced

Directions:

1) Preheat the air fryer to 360°F for five minutes.

2) Place in a bowl all ingredients. Give a good stir to coat the chicken with the seasonings.

3) Place the seasoned chicken in the air fryer basket and cook for 30 minutes.

Nutrition Information: Calories per serving: 314; Protein:40 g; Carbs: 8g; Fat:4 g Sugar:1 g

Air Fryer Mustard Chicken

Servings: 4

Cooking Time: 20 minutes

Ingredients:

2 pounds chicken breasts, cut into thick strips

Salt and pepper to taste

2 tablespoons ground mustard

Cooking spray

Directions:

1) Preheat the air fryer to 360^0F for five minutes.
2) Place the chicken in a bowl and season with salt, pepper, and mustard.
3) Toss to coat the chicken with the seasoning.
4) Spray the chicken with cooking oil and place inside the air fryer basket.
5) Cook for 20 minutes.

Nutrition Information: Calories per serving: 220; Protein: 27g; Carbs: 1g; Fat: 5g Sugar: 0.5g

Air Fried Korean Chicken

Servings: 4

Cooking Time: 25 minutes

Ingredients:

2 pounds chicken legs, skin removed

2 tablespoons rice wine

1 teaspoon garlic powder

3 tablespoons soy sauce

¼ teaspoon ginger powder

½ teaspoon sesame oil

Directions:

1) Place all ingredients in a Ziploc bowl and allow to marinate in the fridge for two hours.

2) Preheat the air fryer to 360^0F for five minutes.

3) Place the chicken inside the air fryer. Make sure that there is enough space for the hot air to circulate. Cook in batches if necessary.

4) Cook for 25 minutes.

Nutrition Information: Calories per serving: ;289 Protein: 25g; Carbs: 3g; Fat: 5g Sugar: 1g

Air Fried Chicken and Broccoli

Servings: 4

Cooking Time: 20 minutes

Ingredients:

1-pound boneless chicken breasts, cut into bite-sized pieces

1 teaspoon olive oil

½ teaspoon garlic powder

1 teaspoon sesame seed oil

2 teaspoons rice vinegar

2 teaspoons hot sauce

Salt and pepper to taste

¼ pound broccoli, cut into florets

Directions:

1) Place the chicken, olive oil, garlic powder, sesame seed oil, rice vinegar, and hot sauce in a bowl. Season with salt and pepper to taste. Allow to marinate for 2 hours inside the fridge.

2) Preheat the air fryer to $360°F$ for five minutes.

3) Place the seasoned chicken in the air fryer basket and place. Add on top the broccoli florets.

4) Cook for 20 minutes. Cook in batches if necessary.

Nutrition Information: Calories per serving: 191; Protein: 25g; Carbs: 4g; Fat: 7g Sugar: 1g

Air Fried Ginger and Lemon Grass Chicken

Servings: 4

Cooking Time: 25 minutes

Ingredients:

2 cloves garlic, minced

1 thumb-size ginger, peeled and minced

1 sprig lemon grass

1-pound boneless chicken thighs, skin removed

1/4 teaspoon salt

Directions:

1) Place the garlic, ginger, and lemon grass in a food processor. Pulse until smooth.

2) Pour into a bowl and add the chicken. Season with salt to taste. Massage the chicken with the sauce. Allow to marinate for 2 hours inside the fridge.

3) Preheat the air fryer to 360°F for five minutes.

4) Place the chicken pieces inside the air fryer and cook for 25 minutes.

5) Cook in batches if possible.

Nutrition Information: Calories per serving: 250; Protein: 26g; Carbs: 9g; Fat: 3g Sugar: 2g

Air Fryer Rosemary Chicken Breast

Servings: 1

Cooking Time: 20 minutes

Ingredients:

1 boneless chicken breast

¼ teaspoon salt

¼ teaspoon garlic powder

¼ teaspoon garlic powder

A sprig of rosemary

Salt and pepper to taste

Juice from 1 lemon

Directions:

1) Place all ingredients in a Ziploc bag and allow the chicken to marinate in the fridge for 3 hours.

2) Preheat the air fryer to 360°F for five minutes.

3) Place the chicken breast in the air fryer basket.

4) Cook for 20 minutes

Nutrition Information: Calories per serving: 183; Protein: 20g; Carbs: 9g; Fat: 5g Sugar: 4g

Optavia Diet Lean and Green Air Fryed Vegetarian Recipes

Air Fried Crispy Vegetables

Servings: 1

Cooking Time: 10 minutes

Ingredients:

2 cups mixed vegetables (bell pepper, cauliflower, and mushrooms)

Salt and pepper to taste

Juice from ½ lemon

Cooking spray

Directions:

1) Preheat the air fryer to 350°F for five minutes.

2) Place all ingredients in a bowl and toss to coat the vegetables with seasonings.

3) Spray cooking oil on the vegetables.

4) Place inside the air fryer basket and cook for 10 minutes.

5) Halfway through the cooking time, give the air fryer basket a shake.

Nutrition Information: Calories per serving: 104; Protein: 3g; Carbs: 12g; Fat: 4g Sugar: 3g

Air Fried Broccoli

Servings: 1

Cooking Time: 10 minutes

Ingredients:

1 cup broccoli florets

1 teaspoon smoked paprika

Salt and pepper to taste

Cooking spray

Directions:

1) Preheat the air fryer to 350^0F for five minutes.

2) Place the broccoli florets in a bowl and season with salt and pepper to taste.

3) Spray the broccoli florets with cooking oil.

4) Place inside the air fryer and cook for 10 minutes.

5) Make sure to give the air fryer basket a shake halfway through the cooking time.

Nutrition Information: Calories per serving: 33; Protein: 3g; Carbs: 7g; Fat: 2g Sugar: 0.9g

Air Fried Roasted Asparagus

Servings: 2

Cooking Time: 10 minutes

Ingredients:

1-pound fresh asparagus, ends trimmed

Salt and pepper to taste

½ tablespoon extra-virgin olive oil

Directions:

1) Preheat the air fryer to 350°F for five minutes.

2) Place all ingredients in a bowl and toss to coat the asparagus with the seasonings.

3) Place the seasoned asparagus in the air fryer basket and cook for 10 minutes.

Nutrition Information: Calories per serving: 68; Protein: 6g; Carbs: 11g; Fat:2 g Sugar: 0.9g

Air Fried Collard Greens

Servings: 2

Cooking Time: 10 minutes

Ingredients:

2 bunch collard greens

1 clove onion, minced finely

A dash of salt and pepper to taste

½ tablespoon vinegar

Directions:

1) Preheat the air fryer to $300°F$ for five minutes.

2) In a bowl, combine together all ingredients and toss to coat collard greens with the seasoning.

3) Place the seasoned collard greens in the air fryer basket.

4) Cook for 10 minutes.

5) Give the air fryer basket a shake halfway through the cooking time for even cooking.

Nutrition Information: Calories per serving: 43; Protein: 2.1g; Carbs: 9g; Fat: 0g Sugar: 2g

Air Fried Mushrooms

Servings: 2

Cooking Time: 15 minutes

Ingredients:

8 ounces mushrooms, washed and dried

1 teaspoon olive oil

½ teaspoon garlic powder

1 teaspoon soy sauce

Salt to taste

Black pepper to taste

Chopped parsley for garnish

Directions:

1) Preheat the air fryer to 300^0F for five minutes.

2) In a bowl, combine together all ingredients and toss to coat mushrooms with the seasoning.

3) Place the seasoned mushrooms in the air fryer basket.

4) Cook for 15 minutes.

5) Give the air fryer basket a shake halfway through the cooking time for even cooking.

6) Cook in batches if necessary.

Nutrition Information: Calories per serving: 92; Protein: 4g; Carbs: 5g; Fat: 2g Sugar: 1g

Thai Asparagus, Kale, And Garlic Mushrooms

Servings: 6

Cooking Time: 15 minutes

Ingredients:

1 tablespoon coconut oil

10 ounces mushrooms, quartered

1-pound fresh asparagus, trimmed and cut into 1-inch pieces

2 garlic cloves, minced

½ teaspoon dried oregano

Salt and pepper to taste

2 cups fresh kale, chopped

1 teaspoon balsamic vinegar

Toasted sesame seeds

Directions:

1) Preheat the air fryer to 300°F for five minutes.

2) In a bowl, combine together all ingredients and toss to coat the vegetables with the seasoning.

3) Place the seasoned vegetables in the air fryer basket.

4) Cook for 15 minutes.

5) Give the air fryer basket a shake halfway through the cooking time for even cooking.

6) Cook in batches if necessary.

Nutrition Information: Calories per serving: 129; Protein:4 g; Carbs: 7g; Fat: 3g Sugar: 2g

Air Fried Asparagus Fries

Servings: 2

Cooking Time: 10 minutes

Ingredients:

20 asparagus spears, trimmed

Egg white from 1 egg, whisked

1 teaspoon water

1/3 cup almond meal

1 tablespoon garlic powder

Salt and pepper to taste

Cooking spray

Directions:

1) Preheat the air fryer to 300^0F for five minutes.
2) In a bowl, combine together all ingredients and toss to coat the asparagus with the seasoning.
3) Place the seasoned asparagus in the air fryer basket.
4) Cook for 10 minutes.
5) Give the air fryer basket a shake halfway through the cooking time for even cooking.
6) Cook in batches if necessary.

Nutrition Information: Calories per serving: 186; Protein: 8g; Carbs: 16g; Fat: 5g Sugar: 1g

Collard Chips

Servings: 1

Cooking Time: 10 minutes

Ingredients:

1 tablespoon olive oil

6 collard leaves, torn

Salt and pepper to taste

Directions:

1) Preheat the air fryer to 300^0F for five minutes.

2) In a bowl, combine together all ingredients and toss to coat the collard greens with the seasoning.

3) Place the seasoned collard greens in the air fryer basket.

4) Cook for 10 minutes.

5) Give the air fryer basket a shake halfway through the cooking time for even cooking.

Nutrition Information: Calories per serving: 185; Protein: 7.4g; Carbs: 15g; Fat: 10g Sugar: 3g

Air Fryer Artichoke

Servings: 4

Cooking Time: 15 minutes

Ingredients:

1 can quartered artichoke hearts in water, drained

2 teaspoons grated parmesan cheese

¼ teaspoon Italian seasoning

¼ teaspoon salt

¼ teaspoon black pepper

1 tablespoon olive oil

Directions:

1) Preheat the air fryer to 350^0F for five minutes.

2) In a bowl, combine together all ingredients and toss to coat the artichoke hearts with the seasoning.

3) Place the seasoned artichoke hearts in the air fryer basket.

4) Cook for 15 minutes.

5) Give the air fryer basket a shake halfway through the cooking time for even cooking.

6) Cook in batches if necessary.

Nutrition Information: Calories per serving: 67; Protein: 3g; Carbs: 7g; Fat: 2g Sugar:0.4 g

Air Fried Eggplants

Servings:

Cooking Time: minutes

Ingredients:

1 medium eggplant, cut into ½ inch chunks

1 tablespoon olive oil

½ teaspoon salt

Directions:

1) Preheat the air fryer to 350°F for five minutes.

2) In a bowl, combine together all ingredients and toss to coat the eggplants with the seasoning.

3) Place the seasoned eggplants in the air fryer basket.

4) Cook for 15 minutes.

5) Give the air fryer basket a shake halfway through the cooking time for even cooking.

Nutrition Information: Calories per serving: 70; Protein: 0.4g; Carbs: 3g; Fat: 2g Sugar: 0.3g

Spicy Air Fried Eggplant

Servings: 2

Cooking Time: 15 minutes

Ingredients:

1 large eggplant, cut into cubes

1 tablespoon olive oil

¼ teaspoon garlic powder

¼ teaspoon paprika powder

¼ teaspoon cayenne pepper powder

Salt to taste

Directions:

1) Preheat the air fryer to $350°F$ for five minutes.

2) In a bowl, combine together all ingredients and toss to coat the eggplants with the seasoning.

3) Place the seasoned eggplants in the air fryer basket.

4) Cook for 15 minutes.

5) Give the air fryer basket a shake halfway through the cooking time for even cooking.

Nutrition Information: Calories per serving: 133; Protein: 3g; Carbs: 17 g; Fat: 5g Sugar: 7g

Air Fryer Butternut Squash Fries

Servings: 4

Cooking Time: 15 minutes

Ingredients:

3 cups butternut squash, peeled and cut into thick strips

1 teaspoon olive oil

1 teaspoon dried oregano

½ teaspoon smoked paprika

Salt to taste

Directions:

1) Preheat the air fryer to 350^0F for five minutes.

2) In a bowl, combine together all ingredients and toss to coat the butternut squash with the seasoning.

3) Place the seasoned butternut squash in the air fryer basket.

4) Cook for 15 minutes.

5) Give the air fryer basket a shake halfway through the cooking time for even cooking.

6) Cook in batches if necessary.

Nutrition Information: Calories per serving: 80; Protein: 1g; Carbs: 13g; Fat: 3g Sugar: 2g

Air Fried Cinnamon Butternut Squash

Servings: 4

Cooking Time: 15 minutes

Ingredients:

4 cups butternut squash

1 teaspoon ground cinnamon

Cooking spray

Directions:

1) Preheat the air fryer to $350°F$ for five minutes.

2) In a bowl, combine together all ingredients and toss to coat the butternut squash with the cinnamon.

3) Place the seasoned butternut squash in the air fryer basket.

4) Cook for 15 minutes.

5) Give the air fryer basket a shake halfway through the cooking time for even cooking.

6) Cook in batches if necessary.

Nutrition Information: Calories per serving: 57; Protein: 1g; Carbs: 11g; Fat: 2g Sugar: 1g

Air Fried Swiss Chard Chips

Servings: 2

Cooking Time: 10 minutes

Ingredients:

1 teaspoon olive oil

3 tablespoons fresh lemon juice

½ teaspoon garlic powder

2 bunches Swiss chard, stems removed and torn

Salt and pepper to taste

Directions:

1) Preheat the air fryer to 350°F for five minutes.

2) In a bowl, combine together all ingredients and toss to coat the Swiss chard with the seasoning.

3) Place the seasoned Swiss chard in the air fryer basket.

4) Cook for 10 minutes.

5) Give the air fryer basket a shake halfway through the cooking time for even cooking.

Nutrition Information: Calories per serving: 53; Protein: 1g; Carbs: 9g; Fat: 2g Sugar: 0.4g

Air Fried Roasted Cauliflower

Servings: 4

Cooking Time: 15 minutes

Ingredients:

3 cloves garlic, minced

1 teaspoon olive oil

½ teaspoon salt

½ teaspoon smoked paprika

4 cups cauliflower florets

Directions:

1) Preheat the air fryer to 350^0F for five minutes.

2) In a bowl, combine together all ingredients and toss to coat the cauliflower florets with the seasoning.

3) Place the seasoned cauliflowers in the air fryer basket.

4) Cook for 15 minutes.

5) Give the air fryer basket a shake halfway through the cooking time for even cooking.

6) Cook in batches if necessary.

Nutrition Information: Calories per serving: 41; Protein: 2.2g; Carbs: 6g; Fat: 1.5g Sugar: 2g

Air Fried Roasted Broccoli and Cauliflower

Servings: 6

Cooking Time: 15 minutes

Ingredients:

3 cups broccoli florets

3 cups cauliflower florets

1 tablespoon olive oil

½ teaspoon garlic powder

¼ teaspoon sea salt

¼ teaspoon paprika

1/8 teaspoon ground black pepper

Directions:

1) Preheat the air fryer to 350^0F for five minutes.

2) In a bowl, combine together all ingredients and toss to coat the cauliflower and broccoli florets with the seasoning.

3) Place the seasoned cauliflower and broccoli florets in the air fryer basket.

4) Cook for 15 minutes.

5) Give the air fryer basket a shake halfway through the cooking time for even cooking.

6) Cook in batches if necessary.

Nutrition Information: Calories per serving: 68; Protein:2 g; Carbs: 6g; Fat: 1g Sugar: 2g

Roasted Purple Cauliflower

Servings: 1

Cooking Time: 15 minutes

Ingredients:

1 teaspoon olive oil

Half of one large cauliflower, cut into florets

Salt and pepper to taste

Directions:

1) Preheat the air fryer to 350^0F for five minutes.

2) In a bowl, combine together all ingredients and toss to coat the cauliflower florets with the seasoning.

3) Place the seasoned cauliflower florets in the air fryer basket.

4) Cook for 15 minutes.

5) Give the air fryer basket a shake halfway through the cooking time for even cooking.

Nutrition Information: Calories per serving: 268; Protein: 17g; Carbs: 46g; Fat: 7g Sugar: 12g

Air Fryer Kale Chips

Servings: 4

Cooking Time: 10 minutes

Ingredients:

6 cups chopped kale; stems removed

1 tablespoon olive oil

1 teaspoon garlic powder

½ teaspoon salt

A dash of pepper

Directions:

1) Preheat the air fryer to 350°F for five minutes.

2) In a bowl, combine together all ingredients and toss to coat the kale leaves with the seasoning.

3) Place the seasoned kale leaves in the air fryer basket.

4) Cook for 10 minutes.

5) Give the air fryer basket a shake halfway through the cooking time for even cooking.

6) Cook in batches if necessary.

Nutrition Information: Calories per serving: 49; Protein: 2g; Carbs: 4g; Fat: 2g Sugar: 1g

Air Fried Roasted Tomatoes

Servings: 2

Cooking Time: 20 minutes

Ingredients:

8 fresh Roma tomatoes

1 teaspoon olive oil

1 teaspoon salt

1 teaspoon fresh rosemary

Directions:

1) Preheat the air fryer to 300^0F for five minutes.

2) In a bowl, combine together all ingredients and toss to coat the tomatoes with the seasoning.

3) Place the seasoned tomatoes in the air fryer basket.

4) Cook for 20 minutes.

5) Give the air fryer basket a shake halfway through the cooking time for even cooking.

6) Cook in batches if necessary.

Nutrition Information: Calories per serving: 91; Protein: 5g; Carbs: 14.2g; Fat: 3.1g Sugar: 0g

Air Fryer Stuffed Tomatoes

Servings: 4

Cooking Time: 20 minutes

Ingredients:

4 large tomatoes

¼ teaspoon garlic powder

¼ cup fresh basil

½ pounds mushrooms, minced

Salt and pepper to taste

1 teaspoon olive oil

Directions:

1) Cut the top of the tomatoes and remove the seeds. Set aside.

2) Put in the garlic powder, basil, and mushrooms in a food processor. Pulse until slightly fine.

3) Stuff the mushroom mixture inside the tomatoes. Season with salt and pepper to taste.

4) Brush the tomatoes with oil.

5) Preheat the air fryer to 300^0F for five minutes.

6) Place the stuffed tomatoes in the air fryer basket.

7) Cook for 20 minutes.

Nutrition Information: Calories per serving: 216; Protein: 7.3g; Carbs: 51g; Fat: 2g Sugar: 6g

Salt and Vinegar Spinach Chips

Servings: 2

Cooking Time: 10 minutes

Ingredients:

1 60 ounces spinach leaves, torn

1/8 teaspoon mal vinegar powder

Cooking spray

Directions:

1) Preheat the air fryer to 300°F for five minutes.

2) In a bowl, combine together all ingredients and toss to coat the spinach with the seasoning.

3) Place the seasoned spinach in the air fryer basket.

4) Cook for 10 minutes.

5) Give the air fryer basket a shake halfway through the cooking time for even cooking.

6) Cook in batches if necessary.

Nutrition Information: Calories per serving: 196; Protein: 24g; Carbs: 31g; Fat: 3.3g Sugar: 4g

Kohlrabi Chips

Servings: 3

Cooking Time: 20 minutes

Ingredients:

1 large kohlrabi bulb, peeled and slice into chips

Salt and pepper to taste

Cooking spray

Directions:

1) Preheat the air fryer to 300^0F for five minutes.

2) In a bowl, combine together all ingredients and toss to coat the kohlrabi with the seasoning.

3) Place the seasoned kohlrabi in the air fryer basket.

4) Cook for 20 minutes.

5) Give the air fryer basket a shake halfway through the cooking time for even cooking.

6) Cook in batches if necessary.

Nutrition Information: Calories per serving: 7; Protein: 0.4g; Carbs: 2g; Fat: 0.3g Sugar: 0.3g

Spicy Kohlrabi Fries

Servings: 3

Cooking Time: 20 minutes

Ingredients:

1-pound kohlrabi, peeled and sliced into thick fries

1 teaspoon paprika

1 teaspoon olive oil

1 teaspoon salt

¼ teaspoon cayenne pepper

Directions:

1) Preheat the air fryer to 300°F for five minutes.

2) In a bowl, combine together all ingredients and toss to coat the kohlrabi fries with the seasoning.

3) Place the seasoned kohlrabi fries in the air fryer basket.

4) Cook for 20 minutes.

5) Give the air fryer basket a shake halfway through the cooking time for even cooking.

6) Cook in batches if necessary.

Nutrition Information: Calories per serving: 57; Protein: 2.7g; Carbs: 9.8g; Fat: 2g Sugar: 3g

Daikon Chips

Servings: 2

Cooking Time: 20 minutes

Ingredients:

15 ounces Daikon radish, sliced into chips

1 tablespoon olive oil

1 teaspoon chili powder

Salt and pepper to taste

Directions:

1) Preheat the air fryer to 300^0F for five minutes.

2) In a bowl, combine together all ingredients and toss to coat the kohlrabi fries with the seasoning.

3) Place the seasoned kohlrabi fries in the air fryer basket.

4) Cook for 20 minutes.

5) Give the air fryer basket a shake halfway through the cooking time for even cooking.

6) Cook in batches if necessary.

Nutrition Information: Calories per serving: 36; Protein: 2g; Carbs:4 g; Fat: 2g Sugar: 1g

Air Fried Roasted Peppers

Servings: 6

Cooking Time: 20 minutes

Ingredients:

6 bell peppers, seeded and sliced

Salt and pepper to taste

Cooking spray

Directions:

1) Preheat the air fryer to 300^0F for five minutes.

2) In a bowl, combine together all ingredients and toss to coat the peppers with the seasoning.

3) Place the seasoned peppers in the air fryer basket.

4) Cook for 20 minutes.

5) Give the air fryer basket a shake halfway through the cooking time for even cooking.

6) Cook in batches if necessary.

Nutrition Information: Calories per serving: 21; Protein: 1g; Carbs: 5g; Fat:0.1 g Sugar: 2.6g

Optavia Diet Lean and Green Air Fryed Beef, Pork and Meat Recipes

Air Fryer Meat Loaf

Servings: 4

Cooking Time: 20 minutes

Ingredients:

1 pound 99% lean ground beef

½ teaspoon garlic powder

3 egg whites, beaten

1 cup grated kohlrabi

Salt and pepper to taste

Directions:

1) Preheat the air fryer to 350°F for five minutes.

2) In a bowl, mix all ingredients until well combined.

3) Pour the mixture in a greased loaf pan that will fit inside the air fryer. Cover with aluminum foil on top.

4) Place inside the preheated air fryer and cook for 35 to 45 minutes until the meat is cooked through.

5) Allow the meatloaf to cool before slicing.

Nutrition Information: Calories per serving: 270; Protein: 34g; Carbs:4 g; Fat: 10g Sugar: 2g

Air Fryer Roasted Beef

Servings: 8

Cooking Time: 60 minutes

Ingredients:

4 pounds beef roast

2 teaspoons garlic powder

½ teaspoon salt

½ teaspoon pepper

2 teaspoons thyme

1 tablespoon olive oil

Directions:

1) Preheat the air fryer to 350^0F for five minutes.

2) Pat dry the beef and place on a working surface.

3) In a small bowl, combine the condiments and spices to form a dry rub.

4) Massage the beef with the dry rub all over the beef.

5) Place the seasoned beef inside the preheated air fryer and cook for 60 minutes.

6) Allow the beef to rest before slicing.

Nutrition Information: Calories per serving: 434; Protein: 61g; Carbs: 0.9g; Fat: 12g Sugar: 0.2g

Air Fried Burger Patties

Servings: 4

Cooking Time: 15 minutes

Ingredients:

1 teaspoon liquid smoke

½ teaspoon garlic powder

½ teaspoon salt

½ teaspoon ground black pepper

1 pound 99% lean ground beef

1 teaspoon parsley

Directions:

1) Preheat the air fryer to 350°F for five minutes.
2) Place all ingredients in a bowl.
3) Mix until well combined.
4) Form four burger patties from the mixture using your hands.
5) Place the patties inside the fridge to firm up.
6) After 2 hours, place the patties inside the air fryer basket.
7) Cook for 15 minutes.

Nutrition Information: Calories per serving: 246; Protein: 31g; Carbs: 0.9g; Fat: 13g Sugar: 0.3g

Air Fried Rib Eye Steak

Servings: 1

Cooking Time: 15 minutes

Ingredients:

½ pound red eye steak, fat-trimmed

½ teaspoon salt

¾ teaspoon ground pepper

½ teaspoon garlic powder

¾ teaspoon steak seasoning

Directions:

1) Preheat the air fryer to 350°F for five minutes.

2) Season the steak with the spices.

3) Place in the air fryer and cook for 15 minutes.

4) Allow to rest before serving.

Nutrition Information: Calories per serving: 540; Protein: 44g; Carbs: 5.6g; Fat:28 g Sugar: 2g

Air Fryer Steak Bites and Mushrooms

Servings: 4

Cooking Time: 25 minutes

Ingredients:

1 pound 99% lean steak (fat trimmed), cut into cubes

8 ounces mushrooms, sliced

1 teaspoon melted butter

½ teaspoon garlic powder

Salt and pepper to taste

Directions:

1) Preheat the air fryer to 350°F for five minutes.

2) Line the bottom of the air fryer with foil.

3) Place all ingredients in a bowl. Toss to coat the beef and mushrooms with the seasoning.

4) Place the seasoned beef and mushrooms inside the foil-lined frier basket.

5) Cook for 20 to 25 minutes.

6) Halfway through the cooking time, open the fryer basket and give a good shake for even cooking.

Nutrition Information: Calories per serving: 299; Protein:14 g; Carbs: 39g; Fat: 5g Sugar: 5g

Air Fried Lamb Chops

Servings: 2

Cooking Time: 25 minutes

Ingredients:

5 cloves of garlic, sliced

1 teaspoon garam masala

1 teaspoon ground cinnamon

½ teaspoon cayenne powder

½ teaspoon salt

1-pound lamb chops, fat trimmed

Directions:

1) Preheat the air fryer to 350^0F for five minutes.

2) Line the bottom of the air fryer with foil.

3) Place the garlic, garam masala, cinnamon, cayenne pepper, and salt. Mix to create the spice rub.

4) Massage the lamb chops with the spice rub.

5) Place inside the air fryer basket.

6) Cook for 20 to 25 minutes.

Nutrition Information: Calories per serving: 338; Protein: 46g; Carbs:3.8 g; Fat:12 g Sugar: 0.2g

Air Fried Roasted Lamb

Servings: 1

Cooking Time: 25 minutes

Ingredients:

10 ounces butterflied lamb leg roast, fat trimmed

1 tablespoon olive oil

1 teaspoon rosemary

1 teaspoon thyme

¼ teaspoon salt

½ teaspoon black pepper

Directions:

1) Preheat the air fryer to 360°F for five minutes.
2) Line the bottom of the air fryer with foil.
3) Season the lamb leg roast with the spices and condiments.
4) Place in the air fryer and cook for 15 to 20 minutes.

Nutrition Information: Calories per serving: 181; Protein: 18g; Carbs: 1g; Fat: 3g Sugar: 0g

Roast Lamb Rack

Servings: 3

Cooking Time: 30 minutes

Ingredients:

1 ½ pounds rack of lamb

Salt and pepper to taste

1 teaspoon grated garlic

1 teaspoon cumin seeds

1 teaspoon olive oil

Directions:

1) Preheat the air fryer to 350°F for five minutes.
2) Line the bottom of the air fryer with foil.
3) Season the rack of lamb with the spices.
4) Place in the air fryer and cook for 25 to 30 minutes.

Nutrition Information: Calories per serving: 386; Protein: 47.3g; Carbs: 2g; Fat: 12g Sugar: 0.8g

Air Fried Masala Chops

Servings: 1

Cooking Time: 30 minutes

Ingredients:

½ pound lamb chop, trimmed from fat

2 tablespoon ginger paste

½ tablespoon red chili powder

1 tablespoon garam masala

½ teaspoon salt

Directions:

1) Preheat the air fryer to 350°F for five minutes.
2) Line the bottom of the air fryer with foil.
3) Season the lamb chops with the spices.
4) Place inside the air fryer and cook for 25 to 30 minutes

Nutrition Information: Calories per serving: 343; Protein: 46g; Carbs:4 g; Fat: 15g; Sugar: 0.5g

Mutton Chops

Servings: 8

Cooking Time: 25 minutes

Ingredients:

8 mutton chops, trimmed from fat

1 tablespoon crushed garlic

Salt and pepper to taste

½ teaspoon cumin

Directions:

1) Preheat the air fryer to 350^0F for five minutes.
2) Line the bottom of the air fryer with foil.
3) Season the mutton chops with spices.
4) Place in the air fryer basket and cook for 25 minutes.
5) Cook in batches if necessary.

Nutrition Information: Calories per serving: 168; Protein: 23.2g; Carbs: 1g; Fat: 8g Sugar: 0.3g

Rosemary Crusted Lamb Chops

Servings: 2

Cooking Time: 25 minutes

Ingredients:

1-pound lamb chops, trimmed of fat

2 tablespoons fresh rosemary

½ teaspoon salt

1 teaspoon ground black pepper

3 cloves garlic, minced

Directions:

1) Preheat the air fryer to 350°F for five minutes.

2) Line the bottom of the air fryer with foil.

3) Season the lamb chops with the spices and condiments.

4) Place inside the air fryer basket.

5) Cook for 25 minutes until golden.

Nutrition Information: Calories per serving: 335; Protein: 45.8g; Carbs: 2.8g; Fat: 15.7g Sugar: 0.05g

Air Fryer Pork Chops

Servings: 4

Cooking Time: 25 minutes

Ingredients:

1 tablespoon paprika

1 ½ teaspoon salt

1 teaspoon ground mustard

¼ teaspoon garlic powder

4 center cut bone-in pork chops, trimmed from fat

Directions:

1) Preheat the air fryer to 350^0F for five minutes.

2) Line the bottom of the air fryer with foil.

3) Mix together the paprika, salt, mustard, and garlic powder to create spice rub.

4) Massage the pork chops with the spice rub.

5) Place the seasoned pork chops inside the air fryer and cook for 20 to 25 minutes.

Nutrition Information: Calories per serving: 234; Protein: 40g; Carbs: 1.2g; Fat: 7g Sugar: 0.2g

Air Fryer Pork Tenderloin

Servings: 4

Cooking Time: 25 minutes

Ingredients:

½ teaspoon black pepper

¼ teaspoon garlic powder

¼ teaspoon salt

2 pounds pork tenderloin, trimmed from excess fat

Directions:

1) Preheat the air fryer to 350°F for five minutes.
2) Line the bottom of the air fryer with foil.
3) Mix together the black pepper, garlic powder, and salt to create spice rub.
4) Massage the pork with the spice rub.
5) Place the seasoned pork tenderloin inside the air fryer and cook for 20 to 25 minutes.

Nutrition Information: Calories per serving: 266; Protein: 59g; Carbs: 0.3g; Fat: 7g Sugar: 0g

Mustard Pork Chops

Servings: 4

Cooking Time: 20 minutes

Ingredients:

4 tablespoons mustard

2 tablespoons minced garlic

½ teaspoon salt

1 teaspoon ground black pepper

4 pork chops, trimmed from fat

Directions:

1) Preheat the air fryer to 350°F for five minutes.

2) Line the bottom of the air fryer with foil.

3) Place the mustard, garlic, salt, and black pepper in a bowl. Mix until well combined.

4) Massage the pork chops with the spice rub.

5) Place seasoned pork chops inside the air fryer and cook for 20 minutes.

Nutrition Information: Calories per serving: 346; Protein: 41g; Carbs: 2.8g; Fat: 17.9g Sugar: 0.2g

Air Fryer Italian Pork Chops

Servings: 2

Cooking Time: 25 minutes

Ingredients:

2 boneless pork loin chops, trimmed from fat

¼ teaspoon salt

1 teaspoon Italian herb seasoning

Directions:

1) Preheat the air fryer to 350°F for five minutes.
2) Line the bottom of the air fryer with foil.
3) Season the pork loin chops with the spices and seasoning.
4) Place inside the air fryer basket and cook for 20 to 25 minutes.

Nutrition Information: Calories per serving: 235; Protein: 41.5g; Carbs: 0g; Fat: 3g Sugar: 0g

Air Fried Riblets

Servings: 2

Cooking Time: 25 minutes

Ingredients:

1-pound pork riblets

1 teaspoon salt

6 cloves of garlic, minced

Directions:

1) Preheat the air fryer to 350^0F for five minutes.

2) Line the bottom of the air fryer with foil.

3) Season the pork riblets with salt and garlic.

4) Place inside the air fryer and cook for 20 to 25 minutes.

Nutrition Information: Calories per serving: 288; Protein: 39.2g; Carbs: 6.2g; Fat: 12.3g Sugar: 3.3g

Pork Tenderloin with Fried Bell Peppers

Servings: 4

Cooking Time: 20 minutes

Ingredients:

2 large bell peppers, seeded and julienned

10 ounces Cremini mushrooms, diced

1-pound pork tenderloin

Salt and pepper to taste

Directions:

1) Preheat the air fryer to 350°F for five minutes.

2) Line the bottom of the air fryer with foil.

3) Place all ingredients in a bowl and toss to coat everything with the seasonings.

4) Place inside the air fryer basket and cook for 20 minutes.

5) Halfway through the cooking time, give the fryer basket a shake for even cooking.

Nutrition Information: Calories per serving: 385; Protein: 37.1g; Carbs: 56.6g; Fat: 4.75g Sugar: 3.3g

Air Fried Beef Jerky

Servings: 2

Cooking Time: 15 minutes

Ingredients:

12 ounces, sirloin beef, sliced

1 clove of garlic, minced

Salt and pepper to taste

Directions:

1) Preheat the air fryer to $350°F$ for five minutes.

2) Line the bottom of the air fryer with foil.

3) Place all ingredients in a bowl and toss to coat the beef slices with the seasoning.

4) Place beef slices in the air fryer and cook for 15 minutes.

Nutrition Information: Calories per serving: 333; Protein: 35.7g; Carbs: 2.6g; Fat: 14g Sugar:1.2 g

Air Fried Pot Roast

Servings: 8

Cooking Time: 60 minutes

Ingredients:

4 pounds beef chuck roast

Salt and pepper to taste

5 cloves garlic, minced

1 teaspoon thyme

Directions:

1) Preheat the air fryer to $350°F$ for five minutes.

2) Line the bottom of the air fryer with foil.

3) Score the beef using a knife.

4) Season the pot roast with the seasoning.

5) Place inside the air fryer basket and cook for 60 minutes.

Nutrition Information: Calories per serving: 420; Protein: 61g; Carbs: 1g; Fat: 16g Sugar: 0g

Air Fried Mongolian Beef

Servings: 4

Cooking Time: 20 minutes

Ingredients:

2 cloves garlic, minced

1 cup chopped scallions

½ teaspoon minced ginger

1 ½ pounds flank steak, thinly sliced

1 teaspoon sesame oil

Salt and pepper to taste

Directions:

1) Preheat the air fryer to $350°F$ for five minutes.
2) Line the bottom of the air fryer with foil.
3) Place all ingredients in a bowl. Toss to coat beef with the condiments.
4) Place inside the air fryer basket.
5) Cook for 15 to 20 minutes.

Nutrition Information: Calories per serving: 258; Protein: 37.2g; Carbs: 3.4g; Fat: 9.7g Sugar: 1.2g

Optavia Diet Lean and Green Air Fryed Seafood Recipes

Air Fried Scallops

Servings: 2

Cooking Time: 10 minutes

Ingredients:

1-pound raw scallops

Salt and pepper to taste

2 cloves garlic, minced

½ teaspoon thyme

1 teaspoon olive oil

Directions:

1) Preheat the air fryer to 350^0F for five minutes.

2) Line the bottom of the air fryer with foil.

3) Place all ingredients in a bowl and toss to coat the scallops with the seasoning.

4) Place inside the air fryer basket and cook for 10 minutes.

5) Halfway through the cooking time, give the air fryer basket a shake.

Nutrition Information: Calories per serving: 190; Protein: 28g; Carbs: 10.34g; Fat: 4g Sugar: 1.3g

Air Fried Salmon

Servings: 2

Cooking Time: 15 minutes

Ingredients:

2 salmon fillets

2 teaspoons paprika powder

Salt and pepper to taste

Cooking spray

Lemon wedges

Directions:

1) Preheat the air fryer to 350^0F for five minutes.
2) Line the bottom of the air fryer with foil.
3) Season the salmon fillets with paprika, salt, and pepper. Spray with cooking oil.
4) Place inside the air fryer basket and cook for 15 minutes.
5) Halfway through the cooking time, flip the salmon for even cooking.
6) Serve with lemon wedges.

Nutrition Information: Calories per serving: 288; Protein: 28g; Carbs: 1g; Fat: 10g Sugar: 0g

Air Fryer Cajun Crab Legs

Servings: 2

Cooking Time: 8 minutes

Ingredients:

1 cluster crab legs

1 tablespoon Cajun seasoning

Cooking spray

Directions:

1) Preheat the air fryer to $350°F$ for five minutes.
2) Line the bottom of the air fryer with foil.
3) Place the crab legs and Cajun seasoning in a bowl and toss to coat.
4) Spray with cooking oil.
5) Place inside the air fryer basket and cook for 8 minutes.

Nutrition Information: Calories per serving: 210; Protein: 45g; Carbs: 1g; Fat: 6g Sugar: 0g

Air Fried Crab Cakes

Servings: 5

Cooking Time: 15 minutes

Ingredients:

8 ounces crab meat

¼ cup red bell pepper, chopped

2 green onions, chopped

2 egg whites, beaten

1 tablespoon Dijon mustard

1 teaspoon old bay seasoning

½ cup grated rutabaga, squeezed to remove excess liquid

Directions:

1) Place all ingredients in a bowl and mix until well-combined.
2) Form patties with your hand and place inside the fridge to set for 2 hours.
3) Once ready to cook, preheat the air fryer to 350°F for five minutes.
4) Place the crab cakes in the air fryer basket and cook for 15 minutes.
5) Cook in batches if necessary.

Nutrition Information: Calories per serving: 165; Protein: 19.3g; Carbs: 20.8g; Fat:1.6 g Sugar: 2g

Air Fried Blackened Flounder

Servings: 4

Cooking Time: 10 minutes

Ingredients:

2 pounds flounder filets

4 tablespoons blackening spice

Cooking spray

Directions:

1) Preheat the air fryer to $350°F$ for five minutes.

2) Season the flounder filets with the blackening spice and spray with cooking oil.

3) Place inside the air fryer basket and cook for 10 minutes.

4) Cook in batches if necessary.

Nutrition Information: Calories per serving: 160; Protein: 16g; Carbs: 16g; Fat: 5g Sugar: 6g

Air Fried Tuna Steaks

Servings: 6

Cooking Time: 15 minutes

Ingredients:

6 ounces boneless yellowfin tuna steaks

1 teaspoon ginger extract

1 teaspoon sesame oil

½ teaspoon vinegar

Cooking spray

Directions:

1) Preheat the air fryer to 350°F for five minutes.

2) Place the tuna steaks, ginger extract, sesame oil, and vinegar in a bowl. Allow the tuna to marinate for 30 minutes in the fridge.

3) Take tuna out of the marinade. Spray with cooking oil.

4) Place inside the air fryer basket and cook for 15 minutes.

Nutrition Information: Calories per serving: 73; Protein: 8g; Carbs: 0.1g; Fat: 4g; Sugar: 0g

Simple Air Fried Tuna Steak

Servings: 2

Cooking Time: 15 minutes

Ingredients:

12-ounce Ahi Tuna steak

1 tablespoon olive oil

Salt and pepper to taste

Directions:

1) Preheat the air fryer to 350°F for five minutes.
2) Line the bottom of the air fryer with foil.
3) Season the tuna steak with olive oil, salt, and pepper.
4) Place the season steaks inside the air fryer basket.
5) Cook for 15 minutes.

Nutrition Information: Calories per serving: 250; Protein: 20g; Carbs: 0g; Fat: 5g Sugar: 0g

Almond Crusted Fried Masala Fish

Servings: 4

Cooking Time: 15 minutes

Ingredients:

2 pounds fish fillet, patted dry

¾ teaspoon garam masala

Salt to taste

4 tablespoon ground almonds

1 teaspoon lemon juice

Directions:

1) Preheat the air fryer to 350°F for five minutes.
2) Line the bottom of the air fryer with foil.
3) Season the fish with garam masala and salt.
4) Dredge in ground almond.
5) Place inside the air fryer and cook for 15 minutes.
6) Cook in baches if necessary.
7) Drizzle with lemon juice before serving.

Nutrition Information: Calories per serving: 379; Protein: 42.2g; Carbs: 0.4g; Fat: 22g Sugar: 0.1g

Thai-Style Fish Fillet

Servings: 2

Cooking Time: 10 minutes

Ingredients:

2 fish fillets, any fish

1 tablespoon minced garlic

½ teaspoon lime juice

2 teaspoons fish sauce

¼ teaspoon red pepper flakes

2 tablespoons chopped cilantro, more for garnish

Directions:

1) Preheat the air fryer to 350°F for five minutes.
2) Place all ingredients in a bowl and marinate the fish for 30 minutes.
3) Place inside the air fryer basket and cook for 10 minutes.
4) Serve with more cilantro.

Nutrition Information: Calories per serving: 195; Protein: 21.4g; Carbs: 2.3g; Fat: 11g Sugar: 0.6g

Ginger Tuna Steak with Charred Green Scallions

Servings: 2

Cooking Time: 15 minutes

Ingredients:

2 tuna steaks

Salt and pepper to taste

1 teaspoon lemon juice

2 tablespoons ginger extract

2 tablespoons minced garlic

2 bunches green onions

4 scallions, peeled and halved

Cooking spray

Directions:

1) Preheat the air fryer to 350^0F for five minutes.

2) Line the bottom of the air fryer with foil.

3) Season he tuna steaks with salt, pepper, lemon juice, ginger extract, and minced garlic.

4) Place inside the air fryer basket together with the green onions and scallions. Spray with cooking oil.

5) Cook for 15 minutes.

Nutrition Information: Calories per serving: 363; Protein: 54.7g; Carbs: 8.4g; Fat: 11.3g; Sugar: 2.1g

Air Fried Roasted Tuna with Dill

Servings: 2

Cooking Time: 15 minutes

Ingredients:

1-pound tuna belly, cleaned

1 teaspoon olive oil

2 tablespoons lime juice

½ teaspoon garlic powder

1 teaspoon chopped dill weed

Salt and pepper to taste

Directions:

1) Preheat the air fryer to 350^0F for five minutes.

2) Season the tuna belly with olive oil, lime juice, garlic powder, dill weed, salt, and pepper.

3) Place the seasoned tuna belly inside the air fryer and cook for 15 minutes.

Nutrition Information: Calories per serving: 232; Protein: 44.8g; Carbs: 4.3g; Fat: 4.5g Sugar: 1.4g

Air Fried Lemon Pepper Shrimps

Servings: 2

Cooking Time: 10 minutes

Ingredients:

1 teaspoon olive oil

1 lemon, juiced

1 teaspoon lemon pepper

¼ teaspoon paprika

¼ teaspoon garlic powder

12 ounces uncooked shrimps, peeled and deveined

Lemon slices for garnish

Directions:

1) Preheat the air fryer to 350°F for five minutes.

2) Line the bottom of the air fryer with foil.

3) Place in the bowl the olive oil, lemon juice, lemon pepper, paprika, garlic powder, and uncooked shrimps. Toss to coat the shrimps with the seasoning.

4) Place inside the air fryer basket and cook for 10 minutes.

5) Give the air fryer a shake halfway through the cooking time for even cooking.

6) Serve with lemon slices

Nutrition Information: Calories per serving: 215; Protein: 29g; Carbs: 7g; Fat: 4g Sugar: 0.7g

Air Fryer Spicy Garlic Shrimps with Lemon and Dill

Servings: 2

Cooking Time: 10 minutes

Ingredients:

1-pound raw shrimps, peeled and deveined

¼ teaspoon garlic powder

Salt and pepper to taste

2 tablespoons chopped dill

Juice from ½ lemon

1 teaspoon red pepper flakes

Cooking spray

Directions:

1) Preheat the air fryer to 350°F for five minutes.

2) Line the bottom of the air fryer with foil.

3) Place the shrimps, garlic powder, salt, pepper, dill, lemon juice, and red pepper flakes in a bowl. Toss to coat.

4) Place the shrimps in the air fryer and spray with cooking oil.

5) Cook for 10 minutes and give the air fryer basket a good shake halfway through the cooking time for even cooking.

Nutrition Information: Calories per serving: 164; Protein: 31g; Carbs: 1g; Fat: 3g Sugar: 0.3g

Air Fried Blackened Tilapia

Servings: 4

Cooking Time: 15 minutes

Ingredients:

2 tablespoons paprika

1 teaspoon dried oregano

1 teaspoon garlic powder

½ teaspoon cumin powder

¼ teaspoon cayenne pepper

1 teaspoon salt

4 6 ounces tilapia fillets

Cooking spray

Directions:

1) Preheat the air fryer to 350°F for five minutes.

2) In a bowl, combine the paprika, oregano, garlic powder, cumin powder, cayenne pepper, and salt. Mix to create a dry rub.

3) Season the tilapia fillets with the dry rub.

4) Spray with cooking oil and place inside the air fryer basket.

5) Cook for 15 minutes until flaky.

Nutrition Information: Calories per serving: 178; Protein: 35g; Carbs: 3g; Fat: 3g Sugar: 0.4g

Air Fryer Cod

Servings: 6

Cooking Time: 10 minutes

Ingredients:

2 cups Cajun seasoning

1 teaspoon smoked paprika

½ teaspoon garlic powder

1/8 teaspoon salt

A dash of ground black pepper

6 pieces cod fillets

1 teaspoon oil for brushing

Directions:

1) Preheat the air fryer to 360^0F for five minutes.

2) Mix in a bowl the Cajun seasoning, smoked paprika, garlic powder, salt, and black pepper. Brush the cod fillets with oil and dredge in the spice rub.

3) Place inside the air fryer basket and cook for 10 minutes until flaky.

4) Cook in batches if necessary.

Nutrition Information: Calories per serving: 212; Protein: 44g; Carbs: 2g; Fat: 3g Sugar:0.8 g

Air Fried Halibut

Servings: 1

Cooking Time: 10 minutes

Ingredients:

1 medium halibut fillet

1 teaspoon seasoning salt

1 teaspoon ground black pepper

1 tablespoon yellow mustard

1 teaspoon olive oil

Directions:

1) Preheat the air fryer to 360°F for five minutes.

2) Season the halibut fillet with salt, pepper, and mustard. Brush with olive oil.

3) Place inside the air fryer and cook for 10 minutes or until the fish is flaky.

Nutrition Information: Calories per serving: 303; Protein: 20.4g; Carbs: 10.4g; Fat: 20.2g Sugar: 0.4g

Air Fried White Fish with Garlic and Lemon En Papillote

Servings: 2

Cooking Time: 10 minutes

Ingredients:

12 ounces tilapia fillets or any white fish

½ teaspoon garlic powder

½ teaspoon lemon pepper seasoning

Salt and pepper to taste

Fresh chopped parsley

Lemon wedges, seeds removed

Green scallions

Directions:

1) Preheat the air fryer to 360°F for five minutes.

2) Place the tilapia fish fillets in a large parchment paper.

3) Season with garlic powder, lemon pepper seasoning, salt, paper, parsley, lemon wedges, and green scallions.

4) Fold the parchment paper over the fish and fold the edges.

5) Place inside the air fryer and cook for 10 minutes.

Nutrition Information: Calories per serving: 199; Protein: 34g; Carbs: 5g; Fat: 1g Sugar: 2g

Air Fried Crispy Fish Skins

Servings: 2

Cooking Time: 20 minutes

Ingredients:

200g salmon skin

½ teaspoon salt

½ teaspoon black pepper

1 teaspoon oil

Directions:

1) Preheat the air fryer to 360^0F for five minutes.

2) Place all ingredients in a bowl and toss to coat the salmon skin with the seasonings.

3) Place several salmon skin in the air fryer basket. To maximize the space, place a skewer basket inside. Place salmon skin on the skewer basket.

4) Cook for 15 to 20 minutes.

5) Cook in batches if necessary.

Nutrition Information: Calories per serving: 180; Protein: 26.4g; Carbs: 0.5g; Fat: 8.1g Sugar: 0g

Thai Grilled Fish

Servings: 3

Cooking Time: 15 minutes

Ingredients:

1 large stalk lemon grass, chopped

3 tilapia fillets

1 teaspoon olive oil

Salt and pepper to taste

1 tablespoon lime juice

1 teaspoon bird's eye chili, chopped

Directions:

1) Preheat the air fryer to 360^0F for five minutes.
2) Place half of the lemon grass on a large aluminum foil.
3) Place the tilapia fillets on top and season with salt and pepper.
4) Drizzle lime juice on top and bird's eye chili.
5) Fold the aluminum foil and crimp the edges.
6) Place inside the air fryer and cook for 15 minutes.
7) Garnish with chopped cilantro

Nutrition Information: Calories per serving: 132; Protein: 24g; Carbs: 2g; Fat: 4g Sugar: 0.9g

Air Fried Fish Fillets with Basil and Garlic Puree

Servings: 2

Cooking Time: 15 minutes

Ingredients:

1 teaspoon paprika

½ teaspoon garlic powder

½ teaspoon black pepper

1 cup basil leaves

4 cloves of garlic

1 teaspoon olive oil

Salt to taste

1-pound fish fillets

Directions:

1) Preheat the air fryer to 360°F for five minutes.

2) Place the paprika, garlic powder black pepper, basil leaves, garlic cloves, olive oil, and salt. Pulse until smooth.

3) Place one fish on the center of an aluminum sheet. Pour two tablespoon of the puree over the fish. Fold the aluminum foil and crimp the edges.

4) Do the same thing to the other fish fillets.

5) Place inside the air fryer and cook for 15 minutes.

Nutrition Information: Calories per serving: 450; Protein: 45.8g; Carbs: 4g; Fat: 16.9g Sugar: 0.2g

Optavia Diet Air Fryer Fueling Recipes

Mustard Chicken Nuggets

Servings: 2

Cooking Time: 20 minutes

Ingredients:

12-ounce boneless chicken breasts, cubed

2 egg whites, beaten

2 sachets Optavia Essential Honey Mustard & Onion Sticks, crushed

Cooking spray

¼ cup low fat Greek yogurt

2 teaspoons spicy mustard

¼ teaspoon garlic powder

Directions:

1) Preheat the air fryer to 350°F for five minutes.
2) Place the chicken breasts in a bowl. Place the beaten egg whites in another bowl and the crushed Optavia Essential Honey Mustard & Onion Sticks in another bowl.
3) Dip the chicken cubes in the egg whites and dredge in the crushed Optavia Essential Honey Mustard & Onion Sticks.
4) Spray with cooking oil.
5) Place inside the air fryer and cook for 20 minutes until golden. Flip halfway through the cooking time for even cooking.
6) Meanwhile, combine the yogurt, mustard, and garlic powder in a bowl.
7) Serve the chicken nuggets with the sauce.

Nutrition Information: Calories per serving: 381; Protein: 42g; Carbs: 3.3g; Fat: 15g Sugar: 3g

Smashed Potato Grilled Cheese

Servings: 2

Cooking Time: 20 minutes

Ingredients:

2 sachets Optavia Essential Smashed Potatoes

1 cup water

1 cup reduced-fat shredded cheese of your choice

Directions:

1) Preheat the air fryer to 350^0F for five minutes.

2) Place in an oven dish the Optavia Essential Smashed Potatoes and water. Mix until well-combined. Top with cheese of your choice. Cover the dish with aluminum foil.

3) Place inside the air fryer and cook for 20 minutes.

Nutrition Information: Calories per serving: 364; Protein: 25g; Carbs:66.4 g; Fat: 0.3g Sugar: 3.7g

Silky Peanut Butter Cookies

Servings: 4

Cooking Time: 20 minutes

Ingredients:

4 sachets Optavia Essential Silky Peanut Butter Shake

¼ teaspoon baking powder

¼ cup unsweetened almond milk

1 tablespoon vanilla extract

1/8 teaspoon salt

Directions:

1) Preheat the air fryer to 300°F for five minutes.

2) Line the bottom of the air fryer basket with foil.

3) In a bowl, mix the Optavia Peanut Butter Shake and baking powder until well-combined.

4) Add in the almond milk and vanilla extract. Mix until well-combined.

5) Use a cookie scoop and make small dough with your hands.

6) Drop the dough inside the foil-lined air fryer basket. To maximize the cooking time, add the skewer rack on top and line with foil. Drop again cookie dough on the foil-lined skewer rack.

7) Cook for 20 minutes.

Nutrition Information: Calories per serving: 128; Protein: 5g; Carbs: 9g; Fat: 5g Sugar: 3g

Buffalo Cauliflower Wings

Servings: 3

Cooking Time: 25 minutes

Ingredients:

2 sachets Optavia Select Buttermilk Cheddar Herb Biscuit

½ cup water

3 cups cauliflower florets

Cooking spray

¼ cup hot buffalo sauce

½ tablespoon melted butter

½ cup non-fat Greek yogurt, plain

1 teaspoon dry ranch dressing

Directions:

1) Preheat the air fryer to 350°F for five minutes.

2) Line the bottom of the air fryer with aluminum foil.

3) In a bowl, place the Optavia Select Buttermilk Cheddar Herb Biscuit and water. Mix until well-dissolved.

4) Add the cauliflower florets and toss to coat the breading.

5) Place the cauliflower florets in the air fryer basket and spray with cooking oil.

6) Cook for 20 to 25 minutes. Make sure to give the air fryer basket a shake for even cooking.

7) Cook in batches if necessary.

8) Meanwhile, place the buffalo sauce, butter, yogurt, and dry ranch dressing. Mix until well-combined.

9) Place the cooked cauliflower florets in a bowl and stir in the dressing. Toss to coat.

Nutrition Information: Calories per serving: 243; Protein: 12g; Carbs:52 g; Fat: 5g Sugar: 10g

Sweet Potato Goat Cheese and Rosemary Quiche Cups

Servings: 3

Cooking Time: 25 minutes

Ingredients:

4 sachets Optavia Honey Sweet Potatoes

1 cup unsweetened almond milk

4 egg whites, beaten

½ cup part-skimmed ricotta

1-ounce crumbled goat cheese

1/4 cup scallions, chopped

1 tablespoon thyme

¼ teaspoon nutmeg

Cooking spray

Directions:

1) Preheat the air fryer to $350°F$ for five minutes.

2) In a bowl, mix together the Optavia Honey Sweet Potatoes and almond milk. Mix until well-combined. Add the beaten egg whites, ricotta, goat cheese, scallions, thyme and nutmeg. Mix until well combined.

3) Pour into a heat-proof dish and cover the dish with aluminum foil.

4) Place inside the air fryer and cook for 20 to 25 minutes.

Nutrition Information: Calories per serving: 349; Protein:23 g; Carbs: 11g; Fat: 13g Sugar: 9g

Peanut Butter Brownie Whoopie Pies

Servings: 2

Cooking Time: 20 minutes

Ingredients:

2 sachets Optavia Decadent Double Chocolate Brownie

¼ teaspoon baking powder

3 tablespoons liquid egg substitute

6 tablespoons unsweetened almond milk

1 teaspoon vegetable oil

¼ cup powdered peanut butter

Directions:

1) Preheat the air fryer to 350°F for five minutes.

2) In a bowl, combine the Optavia Decadent Double Chocolate Brownie with the baking powder, liquid egg substitute, half of the unsweetened milk, and oil. Mix until a batter-like consistency is formed.

3) Place the batter in greased muffin pan.

4) Place the muffin pan in the air fryer and cook for 20 to 25 minutes or until a toothpick inserted in the middle comes out clean.

5) Meanwhile, mix the remaining almond milk and peanut butter powder. Set aside.

6) Once the whoopie pies are baked, allow to cool and drizzle with peanut butter ganache on top.

Nutrition Information: Calories per serving: 210; Protein: 8g; Carbs:21 g; Fat: 10g Sugar: 9g

Cheesy Spinach Smashed Potatoes

Servings: 1

Cooking Time: 20 minutes

Ingredients:

1 sachet Optavia Essential Roasted Garlic Creamy Smashed Potatoes

¼ cup water

1 cup baby spinach

½ cup reduced-fat shredded mozzarella cheese

1 tablespoon grated Parmesan cheese

Directions:

1) Preheat the air fryer to 350°F for five minutes.

2) Prepare the Optavia Essential Roasted Garlic Creamy Smashed Potatoes by mixing with water until a thick paste is formed.

3) Place the mixture in a heat-proof dish. Spread the mixture evenly and place baby spinach on top. Top with the cheeses.

4) Cover the dish with aluminum foil and place inside the air fryer basket.

5) Cook for 20 minutes.

Nutrition Information: Calories per serving: 398; Protein: 21g; Carbs:53 g; Fat: 12g Sugar: 0.4g

Chocolate Chip Cake

Servings: 4

Cooking Time: 30 minutes

Ingredients:

2 sachets Optavia Essential Golden Chocolate Chip Pancakes

¼ cup liquid egg substitute

2 teaspoons vegetable oil

¼ cup low-fat plain Greek yogurt

2 tablespoons part-skim ricotta

2 packets zero-sugar substitute

½ teaspoon vanilla extract

A pinch of all spice

Directions:

1) Preheat the air fryer to 350°F for five minutes.

2) In a bowl, combine the Optavia Essential Golden Chocolate Chip Pancakes and egg substitute. Add the rest of the ingredients. Mix until a batter is formed.

3) Pour the batter in a heat proof baking pan.

4) Cover with tin foil on top.

5) Place inside the air fryer basket and cook for 25 to 30 minutes.

Nutrition Information: Calories per serving: 167; Protein: 7g; Carbs: 13g; Fat:10 g Sugar: 8g

Mini Cranberry Orange Spiced Cheesecake

Servings: 4

Cooking Time: 20 minutes

Ingredients:

4 Optavia Honey Chili Cranberry Nut Bars

1 ½ cups plain low-fat Greek yogurt

2 egg whites, beaten

2 tablespoons sugar-free cheesecake flavored pudding mix

1 teaspoon orange zest

Directions:

1) Preheat the air fryer to 350°F for five minutes.

2) Break the Optavia Honey Chili Cranberry Nut Bars and mix with yogurt. Mix to form a paste. Add the egg whites and stir until well-combined before adding the cheesecake flavored pudding mix. Stir in the orange zest.

3) Pour into ramekins and cover with foil.

4) Place inside the air fryer and cook for 20 minutes or until a toothpick inserted in the middle comes out clean.

Nutrition Information: Calories per serving: 236; Protein: 10g; Carbs: 17g; Fat: 12g Sugar:7 g

French Toast Sticks

Servings: 2

Cooking Time: 15 minutes

Ingredients:

2 sachets Optavia Essential Cinnamon Crunchy O's Cereal

2 tablespoons low-fat cream cheese, softened

6 tablespoons liquid egg substitute

Cooking spray

2 tablespoons, sugar-free syrup

Directions:

1) Preheat the air fryer to 350°F for five minutes.

2) Place the Optavia Essential Cinnamon Crunchy O's Cereal in a food processor and pulse until fine. Add in the cream cheese and egg substitute. Pulse until a dough is formed.

3) Form six sticks using the dough.

4) Place inside the air fryer and spray with cooking spray.

5) Cook for 15 minutes.

6) Serve with sugar-free syrup.

Nutrition Information: Calories per serving: 170; Protein: 9g; Carbs: 28g; Fat: 3g Sugar: 13g

Blueberry Almond Scones

Servings: 4

Cooking Time: 20 minutes

Ingredients:

4 sachets Optavia Blueberry Almond Hot Cereal

¼ cup ground flaxseed

1 packet zero-calories sugar substitute

1.2 teaspoon baking powder

3 tablespoons unsalted butter, cut into cubes

3 tablespoons liquid egg white

3 tablespoons low-fat Greek yogurt

¼ teaspoon almond extract

¼ teaspoons cinnamon

Directions:

1) Preheat the air fryer to 350°F for five minutes.

2) Line the bottom of the air fryer basket with parchment paper.

3) Place the first four ingredients in a food processor and pulse until well-combined.

4) Add in the rest of the ingredients except the cinnamon and pulse until a dough is created.

5) Place the dough on a cool working surface and roll using a rolling pin.

6) Make sure that the dough is ½ inch thick.

7) Cut six circles into the dough and sprinkle with cinnamon.

8) Place inside the air fryer and bake for 20 minutes or until golden.

Nutrition Information: Calories per serving: 249; Protein: 6g; Carbs: 27g; Fat: 14g Sugar: 11g

Sweet Potato Pecan Muffins

Servings: 4

Cooking Time: 25 minutes

Ingredients:

2 sachets Optavia Select Honey Sweet Potatoes

1 cup cold water

2 sachets Optavia Essential Spiced Gingerbread

6 tablespoons liquid egg substitute

¼ cup unsweetened almond milk

½ teaspoon pumpkin pie spice

½ teaspoon vanilla extract

½ teaspoon baking powder

Cooking spray

1 1/3 ounces chopped pecans

Directions:

1) Preheat the air fryer to 350°F for five minutes.

2) Place the first three ingredients in a bowl and mix until well-combined. Add the liquid egg, almond milk, and pumpkin spice. Stir before adding the vanilla extract and baking powder. Mix to form a batter.

3) Pour into greased muffin cups and top with chopped pecans.

4) Cover the muffin cups with aluminum foil.

5) Place inside the air fryer and cook for 25 minutes or until a toothpick inserted in the middle comes out clean.

Nutrition Information: Calories per serving: 211; Protein: 6g; Carbs: 33g; Fat: 7g Sugar: 12g

Air Fried Shake Cake

Servings: 1

Cooking Time: 20 minutes

Ingredients:

1 shake packet

¼ teaspoon baking powder

2 tablespoons egg beaters

1 tablespoons water

1 tablespoon reduced-fat cream cheese

½ packet Splenda

Directions:

1) Preheat the air fryer to 350^0F for five minutes.

2) Mix all ingredients in a bowl. Mix until well-combined.

3) Pour into a muffin cup and cover with foil.

4) Place inside the air fryer and cook for 20 minutes.

Nutrition Information: Calories per serving: 271; Protein: 8g; Carbs: 19g; Fat: 8g Sugar: 13g

Pumpkin Chocolate Cheesecake

Servings: 1

Cooking Time: 60 minutes

Ingredients:

2 sachets Optavia Essential Decadent Double Chocolate Brownie, crumbled

½ tablespoon unsalted butter, melted

2 tablespoons cold water

1 cup non-fat plain Greek yogurt

3 tablespoons light cream cheese, softened

3 tablespoons pumpkin puree

2 packets stevia

½ teaspoon pumpkin pie spice

½ teaspoon salt

Vanilla extract

Directions:

1) Preheat the air fryer to 350°F for five minutes.

2) Place the first three ingredients in a bowl and mix until well-combined.

3) Divide the brownie mixture into small spring form pans that will fit inside the air fryer basket. Press the mixture into the bottom of the pan to create a crust.

4) Bake for 15 minutes. Press foil on top of the crust and place dry beans or rise to keep the crust in place.

5) Meanwhile, mix the remaining ingredients until smooth. Set aside.

6) Once the crust is cooked, remove the foil that covers the crust and pour in the filling.

7) Place back in the air fryer and cook for 40 minutes.

Nutrition Information: Calories per serving: 298; Protein: 10g; Carbs: 6g; Fat:17 g Sugar: 2g

Cinnamon Bun Blondies

Servings: 4

Cooking Time: 30 minutes

Ingredients:

4 sachets Optavia Cinnamon Cream Cheese Swirl Cake

½ teaspoon cinnamon

½ teaspoon baking powder

2/3 cup unsweetened almond milk

2 tablespoons unsalted butter, melted

3 tablespoons liquid egg whites, divided

1 1/3 ounces pecans, chopped

¼ cup light cream cheese, softened

1 packet sugar substitute

½ teaspoon vanilla extract

Directions:

1) Preheat the air fryer to 350°F for five minutes.

2) In a bowl, combine the first six ingredients and stir until well-combined. Fold in the pecans.

3) Pour into greased mini loaf pan that will fit inside the air fryer basket.

4) Cover with foil and cook for 30 minutes. Cook in batches if necessary.

5) Meanwhile, mix the cream cheese, sugar substitute, and vanilla extract. Set aside.

6) Once the cinnamon buns are cooked, allow to cool.

7) Brush the top with the cream cheese mixture.

Nutrition Information: Calories per serving: 179; Protein: 5g; Carbs: 5g; Fat: 16g Sugar: 4g